PREDATORS

BULL SHARKS

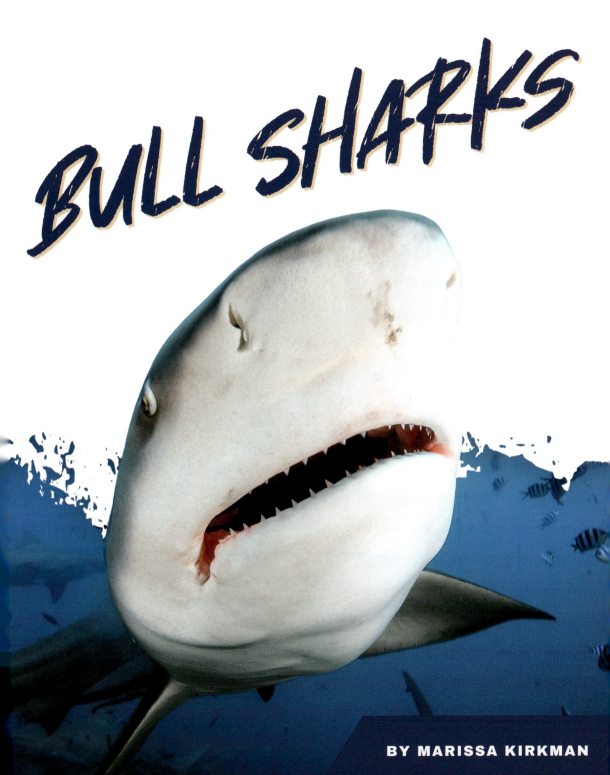

BY MARISSA KIRKMAN

WWW.APEXEDITIONS.COM

Copyright © 2024 by Apex Editions, Mendota Heights, MN 55120. All rights reserved. No part of this book may be reproduced or utilized in any form or by any means without written permission from the publisher.

Apex is distributed by North Star Editions:
sales@northstareditions.com | 888-417-0195

Produced for Apex by Red Line Editorial.

Photographs ©: Shutterstock Images, cover, 4–5, 6–7, 12, 16–17, 18, 20–21, 24–25, 26–27, 29; Jon Cornforth/Blue Planet Archive, 1, 15; David Kearnes/Blue Planet Archive, 9; iStockphoto, 10–11, 13, 22–23

Library of Congress Control Number: 2023910146

ISBN
978-1-63738-771-9 (hardcover)
978-1-63738-814-3 (paperback)
978-1-63738-895-2 (ebook pdf)
978-1-63738-857-0 (hosted ebook)

Printed in the United States of America
Mankato, MN
012024

NOTE TO PARENTS AND EDUCATORS

Apex books are designed to build literacy skills in striving readers. Exciting, high-interest content attracts and holds readers' attention. The text is carefully leveled to allow students to achieve success quickly. Additional features, such as bolded glossary words for difficult terms, help build comprehension.

CHAPTER 1
BUMP AND BITE 4

CHAPTER 2
BULL SHARK BODIES 10

CHAPTER 3
BULL SHARK LIFE 16

CHAPTER 4
STRONG HUNTERS 22

COMPREHENSION QUESTIONS • 28
GLOSSARY • 30
TO LEARN MORE • 31
ABOUT THE AUTHOR • 31
INDEX • 32

CHAPTER 1

BUMP AND BITE

A bull shark swims near the shore. The water is **shallow** and **murky**. Fish and other animals hide in it.

Bull sharks usually swim in water that is less than 100 feet (30 m) deep.

The shark smells a fish nearby. It also senses the fish moving. The shark swims over and bumps the fish with its head.

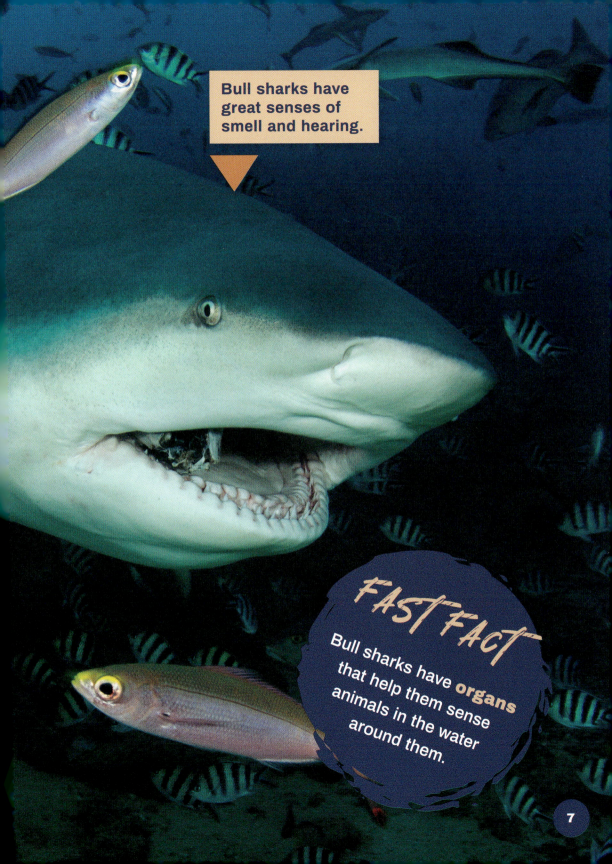

Bull sharks have great senses of smell and hearing.

FAST FACT
Bull sharks have **organs** that help them sense animals in the water around them.

The fish tries to swim away. But the bull shark attacks. Its powerful jaws chomp down on its meal.

WHAT AM I EATING?

Bull sharks cannot see well. So, when they find food, they often take a bite to test it. By biting, sharks learn what the food is. They can decide if they want to eat it.

Compared to other kinds of sharks, bull sharks have the strongest bite for their size.

CHAPTER 2

BULL SHARK BODIES

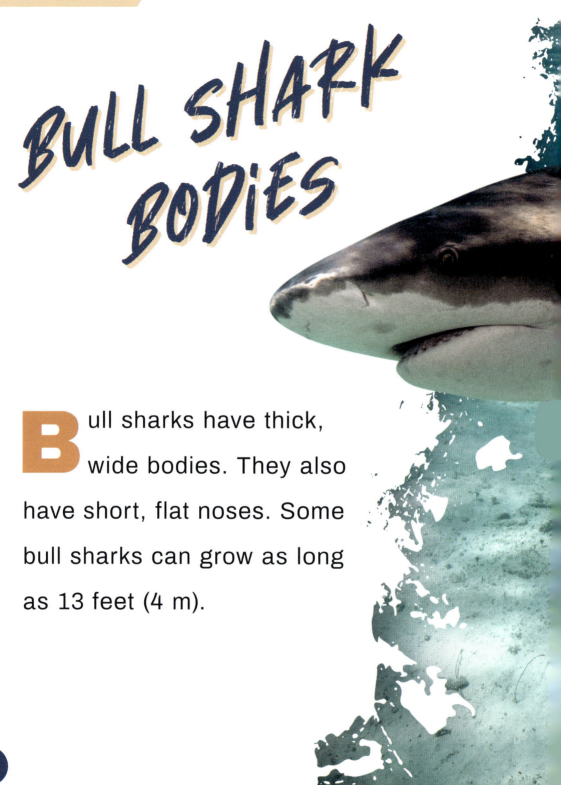

Bull sharks have thick, wide bodies. They also have short, flat noses. Some bull sharks can grow as long as 13 feet (4 m).

Bull sharks usually weigh between 200 and 500 pounds (91–227 kg).

Bull sharks have dark gray skin on their backs. Their bellies are white. These colors help them blend in with the water.

Bull shark males are usually smaller than females.

The scales on a shark's skin are called denticles.

SANDPAPER SKIN

A shark's skin feels rough like sandpaper. It is made of tiny, tooth-like scales. These scales point toward the shark's tail. They help the shark swim faster.

A bull shark's mouth has 50 rows of sharp teeth. When the shark loses a tooth, a new one moves forward.

FAST FACT

During its lifetime, a bull shark can lose and grow more than 20,000 teeth.

Bull sharks are always growing new teeth. They can have up to 350 at once.

CHAPTER 3

BULL SHARK LIFE

Bull sharks are found in oceans around the world. They live in shallow water near **coasts**. But some swim in rivers, too.

In winter, bull sharks swim to warmer waters. They might go thousands of miles.

Pairs of bull sharks **mate** near the mouths of rivers. Around 10 months later, females have babies in fresh water. The baby sharks can live on their own right away.

FAST FACT
Like salmon, bull sharks sometimes leap **upstream** in rivers.

◀ Young bull sharks have dark tips on their fins. This color fades as they get older.

At first, the young sharks stay in freshwater areas. That keeps them safe from **predators**. After growing more, they go out to the ocean.

FRESHWATER SHARKS

Most sharks only live in salt water. But bull sharks can control the amount of salt in their bodies. So, they can stay in fresh water for years.

Bull sharks usually live 12 to 16 years in the wild.

CHAPTER 4

STRONG HUNTERS

Bull sharks mostly live and hunt alone. Sometimes they hunt in groups. Adult bull sharks have few predators. But they catch many types of **prey**.

A group of bull sharks is called a shoal.

Bull sharks sometimes hunt in coral reefs.

Bull sharks mostly eat fish. They can also eat birds or turtles. Bull sharks might even eat garbage, dead animals, or other sharks.

FAST FACT

Bull sharks can swim as fast as 25 miles per hour (40 km/h).

Bull sharks are **aggressive**. They fight to defend their territories. So, people who swim where bull sharks live must be careful.

A bull shark will attack to keep other sharks out of its territory.

BIG BITE

Sometimes bull sharks bite humans. These attacks are rare. But they can be deadly. Bull sharks are so big that even a small bite can kill a person.

COMPREHENSION QUESTIONS

Write your answers on a separate piece of paper.

1. Write a few sentences that explain the main idea of Chapter 2.

2. What fact about bull sharks is most interesting to you? Why?

3. What body part of a bull shark can grow back?
   - A. fin
   - B. eye
   - C. tooth

4. How could hunting by smell help bull sharks in murky waters?
   - A. The sharks could find prey without needing to see.
   - B. The prey in murky waters all smell the same.
   - C. Other animals can't smell in murky waters.

5. What does **rough** mean in this book?

*A shark's skin feels **rough** like sandpaper. It is made of tiny, tooth-like scales.*

   A. bumpy or scratchy
   B. smooth and even
   C. soft and fluffy

6. What does **territories** mean in this book?

*They fight to defend their **territories**. So, people who swim where bull sharks live must be careful.*

   A. places animals live
   B. sounds animals make
   C. actions people do

Answer key on page 32.

GLOSSARY

aggressive
Strong and quick to attack.

coasts
Areas where the land meets the sea.

mate
To form a pair and come together to have babies.

murky
Dirty or cloudy and hard to see through.

organs
Parts of the body that do certain jobs. Organs include the heart, lungs, and kidneys.

predators
Animals that hunt and eat other animals.

prey
Animals that are hunted and eaten by other animals.

shallow
Not deep.

upstream
Going opposite of how the water flows.

BOOKS

Lim, Angela. *Great White Sharks*. Mendota Heights, MN: Apex Editions, 2022.

Pettiford, Rebecca. *Bull Sharks*. Minneapolis: Bellwether Media, 2021.

Rose, Rachel. *Bull Shark*. Minneapolis: Bearport Publishing, 2022.

ONLINE RESOURCES

Visit **www.apexeditions.com** to find links and resources related to this title.

ABOUT THE AUTHOR

Marissa Kirkman is a writer and editor who lives in Illinois. She enjoys reading about animals, science, and history. Her favorite animals to learn about are sea animals.

INDEX

B
babies, 19

F
freshwater, 20–21

H
hunting, 6, 8, 22, 24

J
jaws, 8

M
mating, 19

O
oceans, 16, 20
organs, 7

P
predators, 20, 22
prey, 22, 24

R
rivers, 16, 19

S
sensing, 6–7
skin, 12–13

T
teeth, 14

ANSWER KEY:
1. Answers will vary; 2. Answers will vary; 3. C; 4. A; 5. A; 6. A